HARRY STYLES

LEGENDS ALPHABET

A is for Only **A**ngel.
On this '70s-inspired rock hit from his debut album, Harry Styles, Harry serenades the girl he's got stuck on his mind. She's the apple of his eye, the girl his heart is set on, an angel with a little bit of devil in her. 'She's an angel! Only angel, ooh-ooh!'

B is for **B**oyfriends. Hazza has never been one to shy away from his emotional side. On this legendary slow ballad, he can't quite understand all the crummy boyfriends out there. 'Taking their girlfriends for granted... Only calling when they want company.' Harry would never!

C is for **C**inema.
'I just think you're cool!
I dig your cinema!' In 2021,
Hazza fell head-over-heels
for one gorgeous, incredibly
talented woman. This funky,
legendary tune admires
every bit of his newfound
love, from her coolness to
her movies to the way she
dances just for him.

D is for **D**aylight.
On this track from his 2022 album, Harry's House, the former One Direction star stays up all night thinking about the girl who got away. Although she's gone, Harry remains upbeat, optimistic, and charming. 'You'd be the spoon, dip you in honey so I could be sticking to you!'

Ee

E is for Ever Since New York. With his voice as smooth as it is sweet, this tender tune puts Harry's genius on full display. He wrote it in one night in Brooklyn, just after receiving terrible news about his stepfather's health. In the gentle lyrics, you can hear the pain Harry was dealing with.

F is for Falling.
After his breakup in 2018,
Harry released Fine Line,
an album filled with emotion
and longing. Falling is all
about Harry at his lowest,
drowning in his own tears,
unsure of how to move on.
'What am I now? What
if I'm someone I don't
want around?'

Gg

G is for **G**olden.
On this double platinum indie-pop tune, Harry's more filled with love than ever. He's chasing after his California crush, trying to convince her to take a chance on love. 'I know that you're scared, because hearts get broken.' But with him, her heart will be just fine.

H is for Meet Me in the **H**allway. The acoustic first song on Harry's 2017 debut album showed a new side of him. He's devastated, pleading to a girl he's lost, promising her he'll get better. After years of boy-band pop hits with One Direction, Meet Me in the Hallway showed the man Harry had become.

I is for As **I**t Was.
Haz said hello to change over catchy, synth-pop rhythms with this double platinum hit. The music video, with over 500 million YouTube views, embraces everything Harries love about the star: his fashion sense, artistic eye, and handsome charm.

Ol

J is for Grape Juice. 'There's never been someone who's so perfect for me!' Soft and soothing, Haz's voice sweeps over you like an ocean breeze on this legendary 2022 tune. He's keeping it simple, enjoying a date with his girlfriend, escaping the world, and savoring solitude.

Kk

K is for **K**eep Driving. As a teenage superstar, Harry dealt with more than his fair share of doubters and negative attention. But on this lullaby-style song from Harry's House, he's learned to ignore all the nasty press. Instead, he's going to keep crooning, smiling, and driving away with his lover!

L is for **Li**ttle Freak.
'I was thinkin' about
who you are, your delicate
point of view.' In this 2022
tune, their relationship never
had a chance to start. Wistful
and thoughtful, Harry can't
help but feel regret for
missing his shot with the girl
who might've been the one.

M is for **M**atilda.
In this sympathetic ballad from Harry's House, Haz is the doting friend we all could use. 'You don't have to be sorry for leaving and growing up,' he tells Matilda, a girl dealing with pain and struggle. He just wants to be there for her so she knows someone's listening.

N is for Late Night Talking. 'If you're feelin' down, I just wanna make you happier, baby!' On this radio-famous pop hit from 2022, Harry vows to spend all night—no matter how late—talking to his boo. He's decked out in snazzy polka-dot pajamas, singing over a catchy R&B beat, keeping true to that promise.

Oo

O is for Love **o**f My Life.
If you think the boy from
Redditch sounds like he's
singing about a former lover
on this tune, he is—sort of!
He's crooning about his
legendary home country
of England. And, while he
might not spend as much
time there as he used to,
it's clear the UK will always
be the love of his life.

P is for Treat **P**eople with Kindness. 'I got a good feeling; I'm just takin' it all in!' This legendary, theatrical rock opera is all about something near and dear to Hazza's heart: kindness. He's always cared about treating people well—and he carries that message with him everywhere he goes.

Q is for LGBTQ+
Known for waving Pride flags at concerts while decked out in gender-neutral attire, it's no wonder Hazza's got such a loyal LGBTQ+ fanbase! From releasing 'Treat People with Kindness' Pride t-shirts to supporting an openly gay NFL player, he's always been an ally.

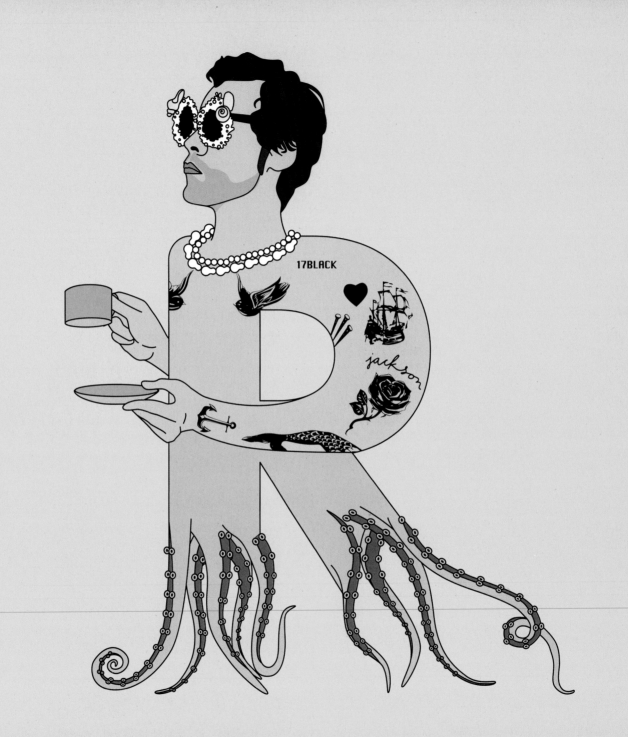

R is for **M**usic for a Sushi **R**estaurant. Jazzy and funky, this song was written in a sushi restaurant during an inspired stroke of genius and is all about pining for a love interest. She's Harry's 'sweet ice cream' and the 'bubble-gum twisted around' his tongue.

S is for **S**atellite.
This space-bound single
from Harry's House starts
slowly but quickly builds
into a heart-thumping rhythm.
It's about searching the
universe for your one true
love, and it shows how
Harry's just like all of us.
He's orbiting a crush,
'spinning out, waiting for
you to pull me in!'

T is for Sign of the **T**imes. True Harries knew how big Hazza would be when he went solo in 2016. But with his first major single release, this 5x platinum ballad about equality, he proved to the rest of the world just how brightly his star could shine. It's also the song he's most proud of writing!

U is for Lights Up.
On this bubbly, pop-disco tune, all Harry cares about is embracing his one true self. He's trying to get past the distractions and break free from his old self now that the lights are on. 'Lights up and they know who you are, know who you are!'

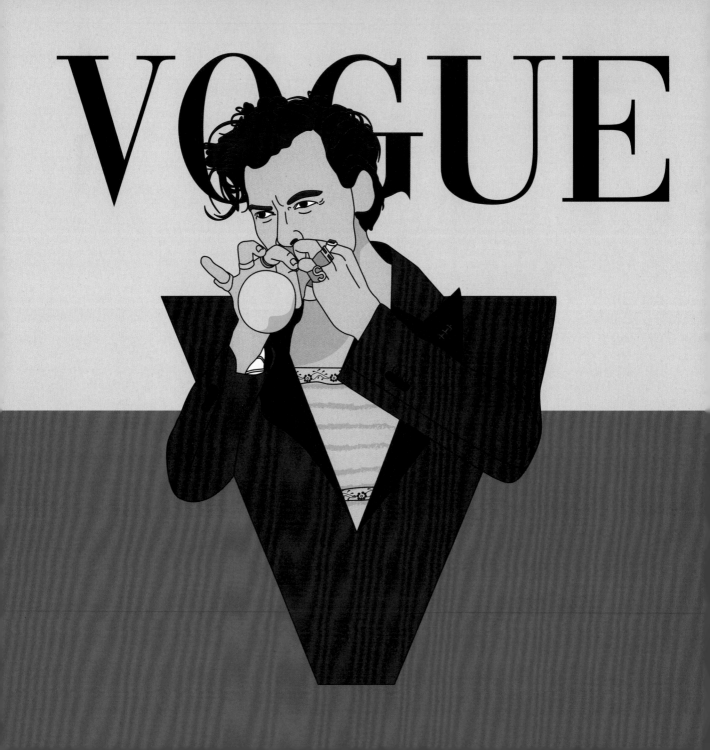

V is for Vogue Magazine. Harry's one of the world's foremost fashion icons, and in December 2020, Vogue Magazine made him the first solo man to grace their cover. Dressed in a black blazer and a flowing white dress, Haz wasn't afraid to break gender stereotypes — and look downright fantastic doing it!

W is for **W**atermelon Sugar. With his catchiest, splashiest song to date, Hazza became the first member of One Direction ever to win a Grammy. It's a light-hearted, 7x platinum tune about the 'sweetness of life,' treating your girl right, and enjoying the fresh warmth of summer.

X is for X Factor with One Direction. Back in 2010, Harry was still just some cutie from Redditch. But with Liam, Niall, Zayn, and Louis beside him, One Direction broke out on X Factor. They finished in third place, but England had already fallen in love with them—next thing they knew, they were superstars!

Y is for Adore **You**.
'I'd walk through fire for
you, just let me adore you!'
It's handsome Harry at his
most charming, telling his
girl that no matter what,
he'll keep loving her.
With its groovy '70s vibe,
this tune became a world-
wide hit.

Z is for Gen **Z**.
Hazza's never afraid to
flip the narrative on its head.
He embraces gender fluidity,
proudly standing alongside
BLM and LGBTQ+ communities,
and always urges his fans
to live and vote with kindness.
It's no wonder this star has
become a cultural icon for
the new generation.

The ever-expanding legendary library

EXPLORE THESE LEGENDARY ALPHABETS & MORE AT WWW.ALPHABETLEGENDS.COM

HARRY STYLES LEGENDS ALPHABET
www.alphabetlegends.com

Published by Alphabet Legends Pty Ltd in 2023
Created by Beck Feiner
Copyright © Alphabet Legends Pty Ltd 2023

Printed and bound in China.

9780645851434

ALPHABET LEGENDS